CW00430796

The Little Book of Men & Women

Allan & Barbara Pease

ORION

First published in Great Britain in 2004 by
Orion Media
An imprint of Orion Books Ltd
Orion House, 5 Upper St Martin's Lane,
London WC2H 9EA

A CIP catalogue record for this book is available
from the British Library

ISBN 0 75286 109 3

Printed in Italy by Printers Trento srl

A woman worries about the future until she gets a husband.

A man never worries about the future until he gets a wife.

Why it's great to be a man

Motor mechanics tell
you the truth.

Your underwear is only
£4.95 for a six-pack.

Chocolate is just
another snack.

People don't stare at your
chest when you are
talking to them.

Why it's great to be a woman

You can talk to the opposite
sex without having to picture
them naked.

Taxis stop for you.

You can scare male bosses with
mysterious gynaecological
disorders.

You don't look like a frog in a
blender when you dance.

5

A female brain is organised
for multi-tracking. A woman
can use the computer, talk
on the phone, listen to a
second conversation going
on behind her and drink
a cup of coffee all at the
same time.

Men can only concentrate
on one thing at a time. They
can't make love and answer
questions on why they
haven't taken out the
rubbish at the same time.

Women don't nag.

Women merely remind the men in their lives to do the things that must be done. If that includes cutting down on beer and fags, it may in fact be life-saving advice.

Men don't nag.

Men assert, instruct, or pass
on their wisdom. It is always
for the woman's benefit.
They think it shows
they care.

Women can talk about several unrelated topics in one conversation and can use five vocal tones to emphasise points.

Men can identify only three of these tones.

Men often lose the plot when listening to women talk.

Women use silence to
punish men.

But men love silence.

When a woman shares
personal confidences with
you, she's not complaining,
or expecting solutions, it
means she trusts you.

Men exaggerate facts
and data.

Women exaggerate
emotions and feelings.

Men value
accomplishments.

Women value
relationships.

Moses wandered in the desert for 40 years. He wouldn't ask for directions.

A man would rather be burnt at the stake than admit to a woman that he's lost.

Men don't get lost, they simply discover alternative destinations.

If Three Wise Women had
travelled to Bethlehem,
they would have asked for
directions, arrived in time to
deliver the baby and brought
practical gifts like nappies,
bottles and a breast pump.
They would cleaned the
stables, made a casserole and
there would have been peace
on Earth for evermore.

Women often use indirect speech: they hint at what they want or infer things.

Men use direct speech and take words literally.

When a woman says…	**She really means…**
We need to talk.	I'm upset.
We need…	I want…
I'm sorry…	You'll be sorry.
I'm not upset.	Of course I'm upset!
You're being really nice tonight.	Is sex all you ever think about?
How much do you love me?	I did something you won't like.
Be romantic, turn out the lights.	I have flabby thighs.

Men's Top Turn-ons

1. Athletic body shape
2. Sensual mouth
3. Full breasts
4. Long legs
5. Rounded hips/small waist
6. Hemispherical buttocks
7. Attractive eyes
8. Long hair
9. Small nose
10. Flat belly
11. Arched back
12. Long neck

Women's Top Turn-ons

1. Athletic body shape
2. Broad shoulders, chest and muscular arms
3. Small, tight bum
4. Full hair
5. Sensual mouth
6. Kind eyes
7. Strong nose and chin
8. Narrow hips and muscular legs
9. Flat belly
10. Large penis
11. Three-day beard

A study in Scotland found that the kind of male face a woman finds attractive can differ depending on where she is in her cycle. If she is ovulating, she's attracted to men with rugged, masculine features. If she's menstruating, she is more likely to be attracted to a man with scissors shoved in his head.

A woman wants a man who is soft, caring, understanding and will communicate, but is also strong, rugged and masculine.

But she can't have him.

He's already got a boyfriend

Research shows that a woman's ultimate fantasy is having two men at once.

One man is cooking; the other is cleaning.

As far as most men
are concerned, no
undernourished waif
could ever become a
real sex symbol.

Women lie just as much as men. They just don't get caught so often.

Don't waste your time telling a lie to a woman face-to-face. It's much too difficult.

Call her on the phone or lie in an email.

A woman will lie to make
you feel good.

A man lies to make himself
feel good.

What men look for in a woman:

A. On first sight

1. Good looks
2. Shapely body
3. Breasts
4. Bum

What men look for in a woman:

B. In a long-term partner

1. Personality
2. Good looks
3. Brains
4. Humour

What women look for in a man:

1. Personality
2. Humour
3. Sensitivity
4. Brains
5. Good body

(Women only ever
have one list.)

Most men rate shopping on a par with having a prostate examination by a doctor with cold hands.

Research has found that the stress men experience while Christmas shopping ranks with the stress levels experienced by riot police.

For most women shopping
is a much-loved form of
stress relief.

Top 5 men's habits women won't tolerate:

5. nose-picking
4. burping
3. body odour
2. crotch scratching.

But No. 1 on their list
is farting

While 96.3% of men admit to farting, only 2.1% of women will ever acknowledge they fart. Men let loose an average of 1.5–2.5 litres of gas a day in an average of 12 farts – enough to fill a small balloon. Women fart an average of seven times a day and emit 1–1.5 litres of gas.

The main cause of excessive farting is talking too much and talking while eating.

Men fart more than
women as women don't
stop talking long enough to
build up pressure.

Women's sex organs can perform astounding feats of human reproduction, are securely hidden away and if unravelled, would stretch over four kilometres. But women never make jokes about them, give them pet names or treat them as a source of laughter.

Women's humour involves
people, relationships
and men.

for example:

What's the definition of
the perfect male lover?

He makes love until 2.00 am
then turns into chocolate.

Men's sex organs hang out
the front in a vulnerable and
precarious position (further
proof that God is female)
and are a constant source
of male amusement
and hilarity.

Men tell jokes about tragedies, horrific events and male genitalia.

for example:

What's the difference between a woman with PMT and a terrorist?

You can negotiate with a terrorist.

The Five Secrets of a Great Relationship

1. It is important to find a man who works around the house, occasionally cooks and cleans and who has a job.

2. It is important to find a man who makes you laugh.

3. It is important to find a man who is dependable and doesn't lie.

4. It is important to find a man who's good in bed and who loves to have sex with you.

5. It is important that these four men never meet.

No man has ever been
shot while washing up.

Men are like a fine wine.

They all start out like grapes, and it's a woman's job to stomp on them and keep them in the dark until they mature into something you'd like to have dinner with.

What do women and cowpats have in common?

The older they get, the easier they are to pick up.

What's the definition of
making love?

It's what a woman does
when a man is bonking her.

How many men does it take
to change a light bulb?

Ten: one to change the bulb
and nine to pin the medal
on his chest.

A Woman's Prayer

Dear Lord,
So far today I am doing all right. I have not gossiped, lost my temper, been greedy, grumpy, nasty, selfish or self-indulgent. I have not cursed, whined or eaten any chocolate. However, I am going to get out of bed soon and I may need more help after that.

A Man's Prayer

Dear Lord,
Please send me a nympho
with huge boobs who owns
an off licence and a boat.

Men will never understand
women and women will
never understand men.

And that's the one thing
that men and women will
never understand.

Men are from Earth.
Women are from Earth.

Deal with it.